Winning Isn't Everything, but Losing is Nothing

Two Powerful Steps to Ensure Business Success

by

Fred J. Lewis

Winning Isn't Everything, but Losing is Nothing

Copyright 2007
by
Fred J. Lewis

ISBN 1-932196-90-0

A WordWright Book

WordWright.biz, Inc.
WordWright Business Park
46561 State Highway 118
Alpine, TX 79830

Printed in the United States of America

Cover design by Renny James

Published by:
WordWright.biz
46561 State Highway 118
Alpine, Texas 79830

Printed in the United States of America

Library of Congress Cataloging-in-Publication Data

Lewis, Fred J.
Winning Isn't Everything but Losing is Nothing

I.   Small Business—Management 2.
        Entrepreneurship 3. United States—Business
        Innovation

            ISBN 1-932196-90-0
            HD 31 L245
            658.022 Le

Table of Contents

To my wife Kathy

Who provides the inspiration for all I have been
and all I will become.

To my father Albert Lewis

Forever young, the older I get, the smarter he was.

Why This Book

Always look out for number one and be careful not to step in number two!

Rodney Dangerfield

Winning and Losing

In every human endeavor, we measure progress in terms of winning and losing, and have done so from our earliest days as a species to keep track of our successes and failures. The first humans had to win out over a hostile environment to survive. They defined success as finding water, food, shelter, and living another day. Failure simply meant death.

While in some places in the world finding these three things remain a daily ordeal, most of us face a different, more sophisticated set of

> *The Winner is the chef who takes the same ingredients as everyone else and produces the best results.*
> Edward de Bono

challenges. Our institutions, careers, even many leisure activities lie at the center of the concept of winning and losing. We have developed a whole set of metaphors to heighten the wins and soften the losses: the caveman *mastered* fire; NASA *conquered* space; and the Alamo *fell*. We need to *triumph* over evildoers and leave no child *behind*.

In business we use the same type of language. We measure winning by *gains* in market share, *securing* the big order, and *innovating* the new product or service. And just like every other human activity, a business has a life cycle.

Each entrepreneur births an enterprise full of hope for the future; faces growth against the obstructions the competition places in its path; and matures and succeeds or withers and dies, based on its strengths or weaknesses.

However, one major difference is that few mourn the passing of a failed business. Certainly those directly involved feel the loss. But for the rest of us, we quickly move on to the next product or service that best fulfills our needs and desires.

As business operators, you must recognize the same characteristics in your customers. They most likely will not change their lifestyles if a business fails. And, even if a business succeeds and thrives, customers will quickly move on to new products and services they view as winners.

Now I could be wrong, so let me share some examples. Do you know anyone who:

- stopped flying for business or pleasure when Eastern Airlines and Pan Am went bankrupt?

- started using public transportation because they can no longer buy a new Plymouth or Oldsmobile?

- still conducts business with a manual typewriter and adding machine?

- feels bad that their quartz watch comes from Japan and not Switzerland?

- recently closed their e-mail account so they could call Western Union to send a telegram?

- won't drink water from a plastic bottle when they can get it free right from the tap in your home?

As you look at your business and want to ensure that customers count you among the winners, it's important that you have a solid foundation. To most people, the first thing that comes to mind is a well-thought-out business plan. Then you must consider the tangible assets, a place to do business, capital, equipment, and so forth, plus the hundreds of other details you need to attend to before you can hope for success.

Certainly you must have a good business plan. And you will certainly need the financial resources to get the facilities, equipment, inventory, and other materials to conduct business. But none of that makes up what I view as the foundation you need on which to build your business.

Before you begin to think about any of those things, you need to take a few steps to ensure that you stand on solid ground, what I call "The Critical Core."

First, you need to have a clear understanding of what business you're in and why your customers will want to do business with you versus the competition.

Who are you?
Why do you exist?
What do you want to accomplish?

Then you must define what makes you special. Why will a customer choose you versus everyone else who offers similar products or services?

For your next step, you must assemble a team of people who believe in what you want to achieve and have the skills and talents to make it happen. This makes up the critical core, the bedrock, the underlying strength of your business, that which supports the rest of the enterprise.

I've written this book to help you build that critical core to become a winner and stay a winner. Page by page, you'll find key steps outlined to take, as you give birth to your new venture or want to tune up your existing business, to meet the needs of today's ever-changing environment. I hope it will help you develop a sharp focus on what business you're in and what you want to achieve. The book includes an often-overlooked key element that can make a big difference in your success or failure: understanding your competition and why it's important to them that you fail. After all, you must have as your objective not just to start or improve your business, but to remain in business and come out a winner!

Step 1

Define Your Critical Core

Do not follow where the path may lead. Go instead where there is no path and leave a trail.

Ralph Waldo Emerson

Decision Time

You've decided to start your own business. Just like thousands of men and women each day, that spark deep inside you has ignited a fire in your soul which calls for action. Maybe you like the thought of being your own boss, creating something with your name on it, or doing something new drives you. Maybe the idea that with your own hard work you can create a better life for yourself and your family has sparked an inner passion.

> *It does not take much strength to do things, but it requires great strength to decide what to do.*
> Elbert Hubbard

Making the decision to take action is the hard part, and kind of scary. After all, at the very least, lots of hard work and challenges lie ahead, and quite probably you'll give up your job or current source of income. At the other end of the spectrum, you'll most likely undertake some big, life-altering changes required to bring your dreams to life. Whatever it takes, it's full steam ahead.

The easy part is deciding what business to pursue. You may have experience or training as an auto mechanic, baker, accountant, software designer, or a thousand other things, so you have a good idea what your business will look like. Or do you? Will your products or services provide what your customers really want or need? And, even more important, can you provide them in such a way as to make you a winner in their eyes versus your competition?

Let's face it, people can find only a few unique products or services from only one source. Even if you want to send a package to the International Space Station, you have choices. You can choose an American space shuttle or Russian rocket. But maybe you're a master craftsman who really does create one-of-a-kind items. If so, you still need to think about how you get these products into the hands of your customers, and why they will want them.

As an example, let's take a look at an auto mechanic and a computer software designer who started their businesses with totally different objectives in mind, but ended up winners by satisfying the same customer need.

Microsoft Windows and the Model T Ford

Before the turn of the last century, Henry Ford decided he wanted to build his own self-propelled vehicles. Even before someone coined the term *automobile*, young Henry had an idea about what it should look like and how it should work. At the time, horses dominated the transportation industry for individual and family trips, streetcars held sway in major cities for urban travel, and the railroads, for intercity journeys. Most Americans had not traveled more than 50 miles from their homes throughout their lives.

Into this environment Henry Ford had an idea. Over the next few years, he and his new company developed the Model T, a product destined to change the world of transportation forever. Why? What was it about the Model T Ford that created a revolution? *Convenience!*

Easy to use, dependable, and cheap, the automobile eliminated the need to feed, house, and care for horses. This new product gave the individual the flexibility to travel at will without waiting on someone else's timetable. Dealers sprang up everywhere so an individual could buy a Model T anytime, anyplace. The world of transportation underwent a dramatic changed and The Ford Motor Company came out a winner in the eyes of the customer.

> *The best way to predict the future is to create it.*
> Unknown

Now let's fast forward. For those of us who learned how to use a computer in the early 1980s, you'll know exactly what I'm talking about. Early personal computers had little or no memory, so you had to insert your software, on disks, each time you wanted to use any of the programs. You had to remove the program disk and insert the data disk when you wanted to save your work.

You had no mouse to help you navigate. Those mysterious "F" keys at the top of the keyboard, or a series of memorized commands (i.e.: Ctrl P for print) from your "manual" implemented any actions you wanted to take.

And that manual was no "Dummies" paperback that spelled things out in a simple manner. When they said manual, they meant *Manual!* As I recall, the computer did everything I needed to get done at the time, though not very easily and not very fast.

More importantly, nothing worked together. If you were working on a spreadsheet and wanted to work on a word document, you had to close one program and insert the disk for the other.

Then along came a young guy named Bill Gates with an idea. He wanted to create an operating system that would make everything work together. Along with that revolutionary idea, he wanted to simplify it and make it easy to understand. Microsoft Windows was born and the world of computing was never the same again.

As a result of Gates' innovation, everything now works together and all the commands are simple. As sophisticated as today's personal computers are, most people with a little knowledge can get started without even looking at the manual. When you want to print, you click on the little on-screen button with the picture of the printer. Bill Gates created his own revolution in an entirely different industry, but old Henry would clearly understand.

Just like the Model T, Microsoft Windows filled the need for *Convenience:* easy to use, dependable, cheap, and it takes you anywhere you want to go in the computing world on your timetable.

So, if we could have manipulated the time-space continuum and managed to get our young auto mechanic and fledgling computer software designer together in the same room to discuss their dreams for opening a business, most likely they'd never have thought they'd have had anything in common.

Henry wanted to manufacture cars and Bill wanted to design software. Yet they ended up as winners by meeting the same needs of the customers they serve.

- Help me get from point A to point B (either in reality or the virtual world) easier.

- Give me something I can count on to meet my needs every time, all the time.

- Make it affordable so everyone can take advantage of its benefits.

Henry Ford and Bill Gates used different tools, automobiles and software, to create successful businesses. Certainly Henry's and Bill's exceptional skills at designing and building cars and software played a significant role in making their businesses winners. And, needless to say, a lot more went into the success of Ford and Microsoft than I just described. But time after time, we see business history littered with very talented people whose businesses failed.

Figuring out what their business *really was* versus what all their competition *thought it was* made all the difference. Said simply, they created a competitive edge.

This realization constitutes the first part of the critical core and represents the basis for all the decisions you'll make as you bring your new enterprise to life. While this may seem like hard work, let me share a process that will make it a little simpler for you.

What is My Business?

> *If there is any one secret of success; it lies in the ability to get the other person's point of view and see things from that person's angle as well as from your own.*
>
> Henry Ford

A systematic approach to getting this piece of the critical core is to start by asking the following questions:

1. What is my product or service?

2. Who else has this same or similar product or service available? (Who's the competition?)

3. What sets my product or service apart from other offerings available?

4. Is there something different or unique about how I will provide this product or service to my customers?

5. Why will customers want to be "my customers" versus doing business with my competitors?

The answers to questions 3, 4, and 5 will make you a winner. These answers make the difference between success and failure and help create the competitive edge. The answers to these questions define what your business really offers and will place you above, and differentiate you from, the competition. Let's look to the fast food business for an example.

McDonald's, Burger King, and Wendy's

No one can dispute that McDonald's led the pack in developing the fast food hamburger business. The company grew quickly into a giant. So why would anyone think they could go head to head with this beast? How could you create a competitive advantage and become a winner against such a heavyweight?

Burger King, with basically the same products, took the position of "*Have it Your Way*." You didn't have to accept the standardized offerings of McDonald's. Burger King said they would make your hamburger any way you want it.

> *You are surrounded by simple, obvious solutions that can dramatically increase your income, power, influence, and success. The problem is you just don't see them.*
> Jay Abraham

It didn't matter that you could ask McDonald's to make a hamburger any way you wanted. Burger King traded on the perception that if you wanted special treatment, Burger King was the place.

Then along came Wendy's. Now how could they possibly set themselves apart from McDonald's and Burger King? Well, how about something as simple as changing the shape of the hamburger? McDonald's and Burger King sold round hamburgers. They fit just perfectly on the bun. So Wendy's decided to sell square hamburgers. As the meat hung over the edges of the bun, it looked bigger. Thus came the "*Where's the Beef?*" campaign and the rest is history.

Now a ¼ pound hamburger at Wendy's should weigh the same as a ¼ pound hamburger at McDonald's or Burger King, but go buy all three, place them side-by-side, and you decide.

(Note: Certainly this offers a simplistic view of what made these three companies successful. But it does make the point of how each carved a niche out of the same business by creating a winning competitive edge.)

So what's your business? What will transform *potential customers* into *your customers*? Why will they demand your product(s) or service(s) over all the competition? Find the answer to these questions and you've taken the first step to becoming a winner.

The second part of the critical core involves your organization. What sets it apart? What makes it special?

Defining your Core Competencies

Every winning organization has certain things that set it apart from its competitors; those qualities, characteristics, and skills that make it stand out from the rest. These factors give it the edge and are called the Core Competencies of the

> *Whatever you are, be a good one.*
>   Abraham Lincoln

organization. Every successful business has them, but they differ from business to business. These are the things that make the group you have assembled to operate *your business* different from the group your competitors have assembled to run *their business.*

As you develop your plan for the operation of your new enterprise, you have certain beliefs in how you want your business to operate. You want things done in a certain way. You may even articulate some rules, bylaws, or standards that all members of the team will need to embrace because you want your business to behave in a certain way. Also, you must ensure that the quality and quantity of the work performed meets the level your customers will expect.

This list will develop into your Core Competencies, the foundation for how you will determine who should and should not be part of your organization.

Your *Core Competencies, a list unique to your company*, are what will make you special. Let's look at a winner and what some of its Core Competencies look like.

*Wal*Mart*

Wal*Mart, the largest retailer in the world, got that way by doing a lot of things very well. You can love them or hate them, but they have certain Core Competencies that help make them very successful.

It's not their stores. I don't think anyone would disagree with me if I said that Wal*Mart's stores are nothing special. Yes, they are clean, well lit, and easy to shop. They always seem to have what you want and at a good price, but you could say the same for a lot of other retailers.

No, it's not the products they sell. With the exception of the private brands only available at Wal*Mart, you can buy most everything else at other outlets.

> *We're all working together, that's the secret.*
>   Sam Walton

You can't even attribute their success to their prices. On any given day, you can probably buy any individual item someplace else at a comparable price.

So what makes them special? I can think of a variety of things, but let's take a look at two that stand out to anyone who has ever been in a Wal*Mart or knows anything about their organization.

First, they have an uncompromising passion for customer service. As you walk through the door and hear that cheery voice of the "greeter," until you finally leave the store with your purchases, everyone in the facility is trained to go out of their way to provide attention to the customer. Ask anyone where anything is in those giant big boxes, and they will usually go with you to find the item.

Second, they also have an undeviating focus on financial discipline. From the way they obtain their goods, to how they operate their warehouses and stores, this focus is obvious. They clearly articulate in all ways their commitment to providing the best "market basket" value to their customers. This undeviating focus on customer service and financial discipline helps make them special. As they assemble the group to run this organization, team members must know the Core Competencies or be willing to learn them, and know these Core Competencies make them special. A potential employee might be the most experienced manager of a shoe department for miles around, but without skills in these Core Competencies (and many others), they will never be a good member of the Wal*Mart team.

The Rest of the World

But you don't have to be the world's largest retailer. As I said, every successful business has a set of Core Competencies that makes it special. It doesn't matter if you're a painting contractor, baker, health club or one of the thousands of other businesses. Whether you lead a big corporation or a one-person operation, those winning qualities, characteristics, skills, attributes, or whatever you choose to call them, that are unique to your organization, will help determine your success or failure. Let's take our baker for an example.

He opens a small bakery in a great neighborhood. His specialty is these really tasty dinner rolls. Over the years he has honed his ability to make these unique rolls unlike any others his competitors can make. When you walk through the door of his shop, the first thing you see and smell is these extraordinary rolls, the centerpiece of the bakery.

People come from miles around to get these special rolls to have with their meals and serve their guests. While in the bakery they buy lots of other things such as cakes, cookies, pies, bread, but they come for the rolls. People can buy baked goods in this town at any number of other places, other bakeries and supermarkets to name a few. But everyone agrees, if you want the best dinner rolls you go to this place.

So the Core Competency, what makes this business a winner, is the baker's ability to make these special rolls. Whatever it

> *I believe the true road to preeminent success in any line is to make yourself master in that line.*
> Andrew Carnegie

is, the baker's skill or some secret ingredients in the recipe, it's the key to his success.

As he assembles his team to work in the bakery, he must ensure he imparts his vision for what makes this place a success. First, they must want to learn how to make this special product. They must commit to the baker's views of consistency and quality to ensure that every roll is always the best they can produce. Second, they must share his view that these rolls are the key to the business around which all the other baked goods have less importance. A potential new employee may be a very talented baker, but if he thinks fancy pastries will make a bakery successful and he has little regard for such common things as rolls, he will never be a good employee for this organization.

The Core Competencies represent the second vital part of the critical core.

The third and final piece comes from defining what success really means to you and your business. What are you trying to accomplish? And how will you know when you have achieved your objectives and become a winner?

What Winning Means

No one starts out in business planning to fail, but rather, visions of a bright and winning future fill the dreams of the entrepreneur. However, many times in the excitement of getting started and bringing the new venture to life, people often overlook one key element or give it far less attention than it deserves.

> *A successful life is one that is lived through understanding and pursuing one's own path, not chasing after the dreams of others.*
> Chin-Ning Chu

I understand that in those early days of establishing a business, so much is going on and hundreds of details take so much time to address, that someone may easily fail to focus on this important step.

This part of the critical core consists of defining what you want to accomplish. How will you define success in this business? How will you know when you are a winner?

This piece of the critical core consists of two parts. First, you need to clearly articulate your goals. Then you need to develop a set of measurement criteria to track your progress against those objectives.

Goals and Objectives

As you begin the process of developing your goals and objectives, you really need to give careful thought to what I call the "What and the Why." The "what" goals and objectives may prove easier to identify and establish measurements to define.

> *What I know is, is that if you do the work you love, and the work fulfills you, the rest will come.*
> Oprah Winfrey

These include things like market share, financial plans, sales targets, and so forth. The "why" goals and objectives may be less clear, but I consider them much more important. They articulate the real reasons for starting the business in the first place. They may include financial freedom for you and your family, the desire to create something unique that hasn't been done before, personal recognition, establishing a legacy for your work, and a variety of other things too numerous to mention.

Regardless of your reasons, they represent the whole essence of your project. They require greater attention as you outline the specifics of your goals and objectives. It won't matter if you make a lot of money or build an empire if you don't achieve what motivated you to go into business in the first place. The achievement of these "why" goals and objectives will define whether this business is really a winner.

This part of the critical core requires you to take the time to really formalize the fundamental nature of what you want to accomplish. Further, it requires that you establish some specific, measurable goals to define what winning means.

This may not be an easy task. If you set financial freedom as your goal, you can probably establish some specifics around what that means a lot easier than if you have as your objective to leave a legacy for your work. So let's use "legacy" as an example.

The concept of leaving something behind of the accomplishments of your life's work is certainly noble. But what does it mean to you? If you're a mechanic, maybe it's as simple as having your customers rave about how well you took care of their cars. As an artist, you might want your work permanently displayed at a prestigious museum or a piece of sculpture erected on the town square. Maybe you want to build a successful business you can leave for your children and grandchildren. However you define your legacy, take the time to fully develop these "why" goals and objectives.

The Executive Dashboard

> *Successful people ask better questions, and as a result, they get better answers.*
> Anthony Robbins

Once you've figured out the "what and the why" goals and objectives for your new enterprise, you must establish the measurement tools and controls you will use to keep track of your progress.

(Note: The best term I've ever heard to describe what is needed was developed by Alan G. Dunn and Glen W. Welling who teach business performance measurement at California Institute of Technology. So rather than try to reinvent the wheel, let's use their term: The Executive Dashboard.)

Once you have your new business up and running, you'll need to monitor its progress. From time to time, you'll have to implement course corrections to keep things running smoothly and on track. Think of your venture as if it were an automobile heading down a highway.

How will you keep it in between the lines and heading in the right direction? To get where you want to go, you will need to monitor your fuel consumption, and engine performance to make sure you don't have any problems along the way. You keep an eye on the dashboard to watch how things are going. Just like your car, you need to have a dashboard for your business to follow progress and avoid potential problems.

In your car you probably have some of the following gauges:

- Speedometer – to track how fast you're going

- Fuel gauge – how much fuel you have to propel the vehicle

- Oil pressure gauge – how well the engine is being lubricated

- Tachometer – how hard the engine is working and if it's working smoothly

So if you think of having the same kind of "Executive Dashboard" for your business, you want to establish those gauges appropriate for what you need to know as you head down the road.

Let's say you're operating a health club and gym. What might make up the right gauges for your dashboard?

- Fuel gauge – Membership: Is it increasing or decreasing?

- Speedometer – Growth: Is the business progressing as planned? Is it slowing as you approach obstacles in your path?

- Oil pressure gauge – Cash: Are members paying their dues on time?

- Tachometer – Balance sheet: Do my income and assets have the right relationship with my expenses and liabilities?

Only you can know what gauges apply to your Executive Dashboard, both in terms of how many and what they should measure, but you must establish one for yourself.

The End of the Beginning

Once you've completed the steps outlined above, you will have established the critical core for your new business. As I indicated at the beginning, this represents the bedrock of your project, that firm foundation on which you will build everything else. If done well, it will survive all the trials and tribulations that will occur as you progress through the life cycle of

> *Formulate and stamp indelibly on your mind a mental picture of yourself as succeeding. Hold this picture tenaciously. Never permit it to fade. Your mind will seek to develop the picture.*
> Norman Vincent Peale

your business. If not done well, it will provide shaky ground on which your business will have to rely when challenges appear.

Now that we've discussed how to win, let's spend some time on those forces that really want you to fail.

Step 2

Outclass the Competition

You've got to look for a gap, where competitors have grown lazy and lost contact.

Rupert Murdoch

What is Competition?

Webster's dictionary defines the word *competition* as "a contest for the same object." Mr. Webster further describes the word *compete* as "to strive for the same things as another." In its purest and most positive forms, competition drives the world, the catalyst for all the progress mankind has made over the centuries.

> *The person that turns over the most rocks wins the game. And that's always been my philosophy.*
>
> Peter Lynch

Competition ensures that the strong survive and the weak perish. By strong and weak, I'm not speaking of mankind itself (a whole different subject for someone else's book), but of ideas, inventions, processes, and institutions, all those things we as humans marked with our fingerprints from the beginning of time.

So competition is a good thing when viewed in the context of the world and the march of time. But we're talking about *your business*, the *here and now*, and *your competition,* those forces that want you to fail and, make no mistake, that's their ultimate objective.

What Competition Wants

Unless you have some very unique product or service that no one else can duplicate, you have competition. Even if you find yourself in this enviable position today, surely someone will come up with the next generation of

> *Great men rejoice in adversity just as brave soldiers triumph in war.*
> Seneca

product or service tomorrow. And as surely as the sun always rises in the east, they will have a single objective in mind: to take business away from you.

For their share of market to go up, yours must go down. People will only want so many cars, so much bread, or so many goods and services. Now a team of economists can come into your business and make arguments about population growth and expanding markets, but remember we're talking about your business and the here and now.

And this competition, no matter how positive, no matter how healthy, wants you to fail, for you to do less business so they can do more. Your demise helps them to prosper and grow big. They want the big mansion on the hill and to dine in the finest restaurants, while you end up in a refrigerator carton in an alley dumpster diving for dinner.

While this may seem harsh, it defines competition—winning and losing. If you think I exaggerate, ask yourself the following questions:

- Is anyone at Toyota losing sleep because GM and Ford are having big problems?

- Whatever happened to that A&P store that used to stand on every corner?

- Why buy DVDs when you can go to a movie theater?

- Do you expect your competitors to offer you assistance in any way, shape, or form to help you grow your business? Since the answer to this is probably no, ask yourself, why would they?

How Competition Works

If you're attacking the market from multiple positions and your competition isn't, you have all the advantage and it will show up in your increased success and income.

Jay Abraham

In business, sports or any other form of competitive endeavor, there are two main components:

Offensive Capabilities (Growth)

In boxing, a fighter with great offensive capabilities can throw a great knockout punch. In business, those qualities, characteristics, processes, and products move the enterprise forward. They provide the momentum. These offensive capabilities make your organization special, give it its character, and offer your customers reasons they want to do business with you.

Defensive Capabilities (Stability)

Again in boxing, you can think of the fighter's defensive capabilities as the ability to take a really great punch and keep on fighting. In business, those defensive capabilities give your enterprise the strength of the solid foundation, the fortress you build to give you the ability to sustain yourself from the competitive assaults that come your way.

Seize the Initiative

To succeed against your competitors, you have to begin by taking away their offensive capabilities. Said simply, you need to eliminate or neutralize *their* competitive advantages. Whether product or service, you must figure out how to be better than your competitors.

You must also capitalize on *your* competitive advantages, those things that *make you special and set you apart.* This enables you to seize the initiative, set the agenda for growth, and force the competition to play the game by your rules rather than the other way around.

> *All problems become smaller if you don't dodge them, but confront them. Touch a thistle timidly, and it pricks you; grasp it and its spines crumble.*
> William F. Halsey

At the same time, you must focus some time and resources on undermining your competitors' defensive capabilities. Let's look at the auto industry to gain some insights into how this works.

Auto Wars

Not so long ago, the U.S. auto industry was the envy of the world. They provided the market with a superior product, made by a well-trained, stable, motivated workforce, in state-of-the-art facilities, second to none.

> *Success breeds complacency.*
> *Complacency breeds failure.*
> *Only the paranoid survive.*
> Andrew Grove

So with so much going for them, you have to wonder how foreign competitors forced that industry from a position of dominance, to playing a defensive game, which now questions their very survival.

First, they neutralized the offensive capabilities of U.S. manufacturers. They built cars as good, and some would say better. Then they convinced the buying public that they did indeed have a better product. They changed the rules of the game.

Now, instead of Honda or Toyota touting their cars being as good as a Chevrolet or a Ford for a better price, advertising bears the opposite message. Then as they began to level the playing field in respect to the offensive capabilities, they attacked the defensive capabilities of the big three.

The U.S. auto industry began the last half of the 20th century with the best production facilities and workforce in the world. In addition, they had a dealer network, which ensured the availability of their cars virtually anywhere a customer wanted to buy one.

At the same time, their foreign competitors, particularly in Germany and Japan, had their facilities bombed into oblivion and their workforces decimated during World War II. While this was a major competitive advantage at the time, it eventually became a vulnerability as time went on.

While companies like Toyota built new facilities in their own countries and later in the United States, U.S. automakers had to live with existing facilities, remodel them, or make major capital investments in replacement plants to meet future needs. As to the workforce, the foreign competitors had low-cost employees in their own countries and in many cases opened non-union facilities in the United States.

In contrast, U.S. automakers have a commitment to a unionized, skilled, highly paid workforce, which because of its long-term stability, brings with it the cost of retirement benefits.

The extensive dealer network, once a major asset, became a burden as sales of foreign brands gained momentum. For example, in 2005 General Motors sold twice as many cars in the United States as Toyota, but they have almost five times as many dealers. Over time, the cost of building and selling cars by the U.S. automakers greatly outpaced those same expenses incurred by their foreign competitors.

What was a set of major defensive capabilities, facilities, workforce, dealer network, over time became a set of major vulnerabilities. The foreign competitors changed the rules of the game.

(Note: I mean this only as an illustration. Certainly a lot more has happened to the auto industry in the last few decades than anyone can adequately describe in this short example.)

How Do I Win?

> *Not everything that is faced can be changed, but nothing can be changed until it is faced.*
>
> James Baldwin

The best way to counter the competitive forces that oppose you is to know three things really well.

First, have a clear understanding of your competitors, what competitive advantages they have, and what perceived advantages *they think* they possess. I use the word perceived because you have to know the difference between those threats you really face and those your competitors think you face.

Second, and equally important, know your competitors' weaknesses or areas of vulnerability. One of these vulnerabilities may be the difference between what they think they possess as competitive advantages and what they really are, if they have any.

Finally, have an even better understanding of your competitive advantages. Then develop a plan to make *your advantages* and your *competitors' vulnerabilities* work for you.

Begin by going back to your Critical Core. In it, you identified what made you special, those things that set you apart. Build your plan around those unique strengths.

Regarding your competitors, find out what they *are good at* and what *they think* they are good at. Find out by talking to your customers and suppliers. I'll bet that your suppliers and customers also deal with some of your competitors. Asking questions and asking them often will give you plenty of information. This data will enable you to piece together the competitive tactics and strategies being used against you.

Once you have a clear understanding of this, you can then develop your own plan to stay one step ahead and win!

About the Author

Fred J. Lewis

Fred J. Lewis has an extensive background in both business and people development. His expertise and experiences developed over a successful thirty-year career with The Quaker Oats Company. There he held a wide variety of Sales, Management, and Leadership positions throughout the United States and helped to make names like Cap'n Crunch™, Kibbles 'N Bits™, and Gatorade™ into household icons. His business responsibilities were balanced with a keen interest in finding great people and preparing them with the skills to face tomorrow's challenges.

In addition to this new book, he is the author of *Selecting Stars: The Handbook for Hiring Success.* His seminars on "The Dynamics of Leading and Managing" have been attended by thousands of business people and countless students from numerous companies, government agencies, and educational institutions. He was an Adjunct Professor of Marketing Management at Jersey City State College, and member of the school's Executive Advisory Council. Currently he serves as a member of the Business Advisory Council at The University of West Florida College of Business.

Fred holds a BSBA Degree in Marketing from Thomas Edison State College, and has completed The Johnson Graduate School of Management Executive Development Program at Cornell University.

Be sure to read the companion book
Selecting Stars
The Handbook for Hiring Success
by
Fred J. Lewis

Mr. Employer! Do you want to improve your batting average for finding, selecting, and hiring the best employee for your organization? If so, then Selecting Stars *is for you.*

Edward Ranelli, Ph.D.
Dean, College of Business
The University of West Florida

Anyone interested in finding and selecting the best available candidates should consider Fred Lewis' book a must read.

Calvin D. Thomas, Director of Human Resources
Office of Federal Student Aid
U.S. Department of Education

Based on my years of experience in the military, business, and academic environments, I can say without question this book is needed. Fred Lewis has written an astute guide to hiring future "stars." I recommend its use in classes in and in business by those in a position to select the future leaders for our country.

General Michael L. Ferguson
U.S. Army (Ret.), Attorney at Law
McDonald, Fleming, Moorhead, Ferguson,
Green & Smith, LLP

Index

A

B

Notes and Action Plans

Notes and Action Plans

Notes and Action Plans

Notes and Action Plans

To order additional copies of
Winning Isn't Everything, but Losing is Nothing
and *Selecting Stars: The Handbook for Hiring Success*

Name_____

Address _____

_____

_____

Winning Isn't Everything
$14.95 x _____ copies =   _____

Selecting Stars
$14.95 x _____ copies =   _____

 Sales Tax   _____
(Texas residents add 8.25% sales tax)

Please add $3.50 postage and handling
for the first book and $1.50 for each
additional book   _____

Total amount due: _____

Please send check or money order for books to:
WordWright.biz, Inc.
46561 State Highway 118
Alpine, Texas 79830
For a complete catalog of books, visit our site at
http://www.WordWright.biz